Pebble® Plus

Under the Sea

Whales

by Carol K. Lindeen

Consulting Editor: Gail Saunders-Smith, PhD

Consultant: Jody Rake, Member
Southwest Marine/Aquatic Educator's Association

Capstone press®

Mankato, Minnesota

Pebble Plus is published by Capstone Press,
151 Good Counsel Drive, P.O. Box 669, Mankato, Minnesota 56002.
www.capstonepub.com

 Books published by Capstone Press are manufactured with paper containing at least 10 percent post-consumer waste.

Library of Congress Cataloging-in-Publication Data
Lindeen, Carol K., 1976–
 Whales / by Carol K. Lindeen.
  p. cm.—(Pebble plus: Under the sea)
 Includes bibliographical references (p. 23) and index.
 ISBN-13: 978-0-7368-2603-7 (hardcover)
 ISBN-10: 0-7368-2603-3 (hardcover)
 ISBN-13: 978-0-7368-5115-2 (softcover pbk.)
 ISBN-10: 0-7368-5115-1 (softcover pbk.)
 1. Whales—Juvenile literature. [1. Whales.] I. Title. II. Series.
QL737.C4L56 2005
599.5—dc22   2003025613

Summary: Simple text and photographs present the lives of whales.

Editorial Credits
Martha E. H. Rustad, editor; Juliette Peters, designer; Kelly Garvin, photo researcher; Karen Hieb, product planning editor

Photo Credits
Bruce Coleman Inc./Masa Ushioda-V&W, 18–19
Corbis/Marty Snyderman, 1
Minden Pictures/Flip Nicklin, 6–7, 8–9, 16–17; Mike Parry, cover
PhotoDisc Inc., back cover
Seapics.com/Doug Perrine, 20–21; Kike Calvo/V&W, 12–13; Phillip Colla, 10–11; Masa Ushioda, 4–5, 14–15

Note to Parents and Teachers

The Under the Sea series supports national science standards related to the diversity and unity of life. This book describes and illustrates whales. The images support early readers in understanding the text. The repetition of words and phrases helps early readers learn new words. This book also introduces early readers to subject-specific vocabulary words, which are defined in the Glossary section. Early readers may need assistance to read some words and to use the Table of Contents, Glossary, Read More, Internet Sites, and Index/Word List sections of the book.

Word Count: 102
Early-Intervention Level: 14

Printed in the United States of America in North Mankato, Minnesota.
012011   006047R

Table of Contents

Whales

What are whales?

Whales are mammals.

Whales breathe air.
They have blowholes
on top of their heads.

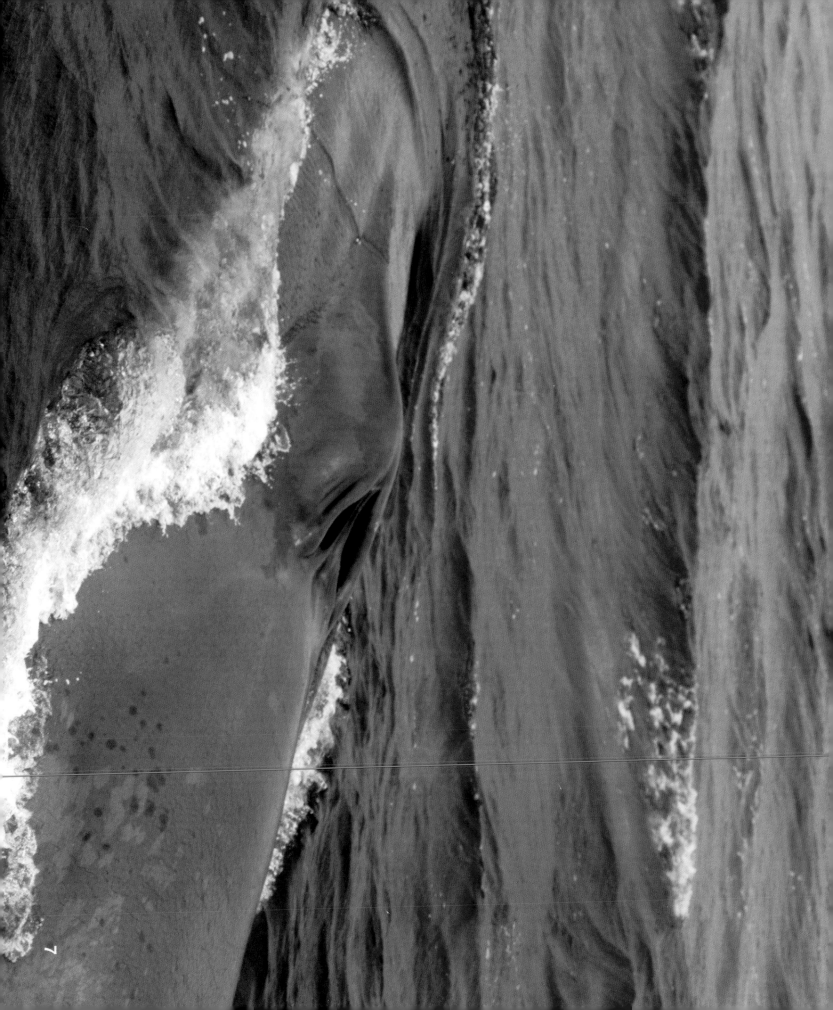

Smooth skin covers whales.
Blubber under their skin
keeps whales warm.

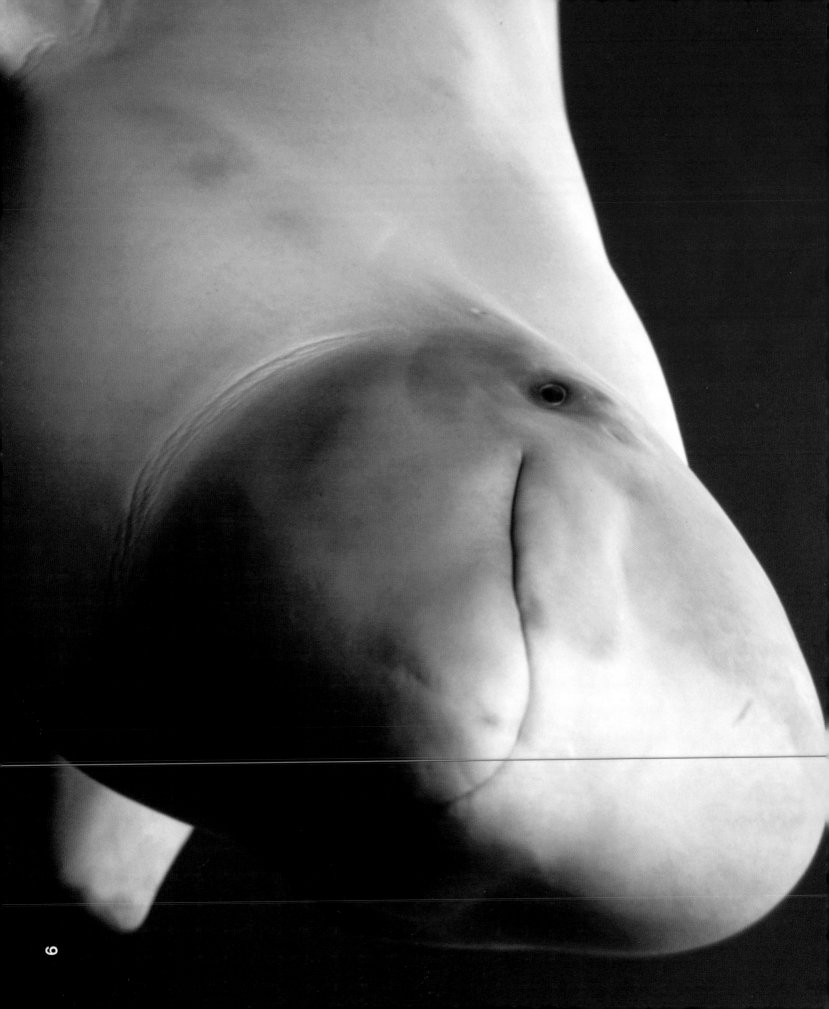

Small whales are about
as long as a jump rope.
Big whales can be the size
of a big airplane.

Swimming

Whales move their strong tails up and down to swim.

Most whales have fins on their backs. Fins help whales balance. Flippers help whales steer.

Some whales swim to warmer water in the fall. They mate and have young.

Whales breach.
Some whales can jump
out of the water.

Under the Sea

Whales swim
under the sea.

Glossary

blowhole—an opening on the top of a whale's head; whales breathe air through blowholes.

blubber—a layer of fat under a whale's skin; blubber helps whales stay warm.

breach—to jump out of the water

fin—a thin body part on a swimming animal; most whales have fins on their backs.

flipper—a flat limb with bones on the bodies of some sea animals; whales have two flippers; flippers help whales swim.

mammal—a warm-blooded animal with a backbone that breathes air with lungs; mammals have some hair or fur; female mammals feed milk to their young.

mate—to join together to produce young

steer—to move in a certain direction

Read More

Jenner, Caryn. *Journey of a Humpback Whale.* Dorling Kindersley Readers. New York: Dorling Kindersley, 2002.

Ruffin, Frances E. *Whales. My World of Animals.* New York: PowerKids Press, 2004.

Rustad, Martha E. H. *Whales. Ocean Life.* Mankato, Minn.: Pebble Books, 2001.

Internet Sites

FactHound offers a safe, fun way to find Internet sites related to this book. All of the sites on FactHound have been researched by our staff.

Here's how:

1. Visit www.*facthound*.com

2. Type in this special code **0736826033** for age-appropriate sites. Or enter a search word related to this book for a more general search.

3. Click on the **Fetch It** button.

FactHound will fetch the best sites for you!

Index/Word List